PASSION UNITED

by

Philip Miles

Grosvenor House
Publishing Limited

All rights reserved
Copyright © Philip Miles Whyte, 2012

Philip Miles Whyte is hereby identified as author of this
work in accordance with Section 77 of the Copyright, Designs
and Patents Act 1988

The book cover picture is copyright to Philip Miles Whyte

This book is published by
Grosvenor House Publishing Ltd
28-30 High Street, Guildford, Surrey, GU1 3EL.
www.grosvenorhousepublishing.co.uk

This book is sold subject to the conditions that it shall not, by way of
trade or otherwise, be lent, resold, hired out or otherwise circulated
without the author's or publisher's prior consent in any form of binding or
cover other than that in which it is published and
without a similar condition including this condition being imposed
on the subsequent purchaser.

A CIP record for this book
is available from the British Library

ISBN 978-1-78148-777-8

Front cover images are reproduced by kind permission of:

"Sunderland Fans 1" Licensed for use under Creative Commons 2.0, (c) copyright Ronnie MacDonald (Flickr).

"Final Whistle" All Rights Reserved (photo by Matthew Wilkinson via Flickr, kindly reproduced with permission) (c) copyright Matthew Wilkinson.

"Causeway Lane Matlock" All Rights Reserved (photo by Matthew Wilkinson via Flickr, kindly reproduced with permission) (c) copyright Matthew Wilkinson.

"Frustration" All Rights Reserved (photo by Matthew Wilkinson via Flickr, kindly reproduced with permission) (c) copyright Matthew Wilkinson.

"Confrontation" All Rights Reserved (photo by Matthew Wilkinson via Flickr, kindly reproduced with permission) (c) copyright Matthew Wilkinson.

"Hoodie Passion" All Rights Reserved (photo by Matthew Wilkinson via Flickr, kindly reproduced with permission) (c) copyright Matthew Wilkinson.

"Ibrox Gates" (c) Copyright MikeyInMotion (photo by MikeyInMotion via Flickr 2012, kindly reproduced with permission).

Foreword

I love football.

I have played it, watched it, listened to it, read about it, and even dreamt about it. I will never stop loving the game.

Anyone reading this book probably loves football too, or at least has some affinity to the game and the pleasure it brings to many millions of fans globally.

Football is a game that brings out passion, even in people who may not normally display it. You need to have passion if you follow a team fervently; even fans of the most prestigious teams go through agonies, ups, downs, delirium, doldrums and even bouts of depression.

It could be that our team has performed beyond our expectations, maybe achieving promotion or winning some silverware. Or conversely, and it seems to happen more often than not, unexpected inept performances or even relegation. Then there are the "seasonal" swings that weekly affect our emotions, a wrong decision, a manager's poor selection, or our once prolific scorer not able to hit a barn door. But if we win, it makes returning to work on Monday more palatable, especially if we have colleagues who are rival fans and they haven't won!

We all have our views and different things affect us in various ways. It may not even be anything to do with our team; we have opinions about other teams, who the football greats are, about obscene transfer fees and billionaire owners. I have tried to capture most things that all fans will relate to, things that bring out passion and set off our emotions.

It's the passion of the fans that makes the game what it is.

I am simply dedicating this book to **every** football fan, past and present.

It's definitely a passion that keeps us going back,
And though it often drives us mad, it's not a fading fad.

We cannot live without it, even when we can't be there;
Whether win, lose or draw, we have to know the score.

Whatever we are doing, wherever we may be,
We think about our team and how they may be faring.

So whoever you support, be they lowly or the champions,
Follow with your heart; they made your football passion.

That's me (far right) with Linvoy Primus, taken after a charity game at Fratton Park.

If you have bought this book ... THANK YOU.

If you are only borrowing this book, why not buy it, it will make a great present for any real football fan you know!

Memoirs, Observations and Football Poems
First Edition

Contents

OH, TO BE A FOOTY FAN!	**1**
HOW IT WAS	**3**
Those Were the Days	*5*
First Match: The Build Up	*7*
First Match: The Match	*9*
First Match: Post Match	*10*
POPULARITY OF THE GAME IN THE 50S AND 60S	11
Passion United	*16*
MEDIA COVERAGE	18
FOOTBALL COSTS	20
Sam's First Match	*23*
THE 70S	**30**
The Darker Side	*34*
Twats	*35*
FAN PASSION	**36**
Saturday Ritual	*39*
Rose Tinted Glasses	*41*
Jim	*43*
DECISIONS, DECISIONS	**45**
MIB	*48*

THE INTERNATIONAL STAGE OF FOOTBALL	**49**
ENG-ER-LAND!	**51**
England's Euro (Dream?)	53
Sixty Six	55
FOOTBALL'S GREATEST	**61**
Simply the Best	65
Edson Arantes do Nascimento	67
SEASONAL SWINGS	**69**
A New Season Dawns	70
Another Season Over	71
UPS, CUPS AND DOWNS	**74**
GLORY DAYS	**77**
A DIFFERENT EMOTION – UNITED IN GRIEF	**83**
Hillsborough, 15th April 1989	84
Fabrice	85
IS THE "BUBBLE" BURSTING?	**86**
Portsmouth Football Club 1898 – 2012 (Pompey forever)	89
The Money-Go-Round	91
FOOTBALL TALK (RABBIT RABBIT)	**92**
The TV Tarts	93
Literally Speaking or Not	93
It's the way they tell 'em!	94
What's in a name?	97
LAST WORD – MODERN DAY ANTICS	**100**
ACKNOWLEDGEMENTS	**105**

Oh, to be a footy fan!

In terms of being a football fan, I am unusual in that I have followed two clubs in my life.

The first was West Ham United, evident in my second poem "First Match". However, within a month after my twelfth birthday my family moved from London to Hampshire. I continued to follow the Hammers and managed to attend about six matches during the mid to late seventies, including the 1975 and 1980 FA Cup Finals (v Fulham and Arsenal).

I should add that my affair with West Ham was just that; at the age of nine I had actually fallen in love with the game, rather than a team. But I needed a team, and West Ham were a top team in that era with three pivotal World Cup stars. When we moved to Hampshire I was too young to be a true fan, being some 85 miles away from Upton Park.

By the late 70s, my London roots were diminishing and I had moved to the Portsmouth area due to work. I had already started to go and watch Portsmouth with my house mate Nick who had been a life-long Pompey fan.

After attending around ten games in succession, we were setting off to an evening home match (v Plymouth), towards the end of the 1977/78 season. We stopped for a pint in our normal match day haunt en route, the Nell Gwynne, and whilst supping, I announced I may as well become a Pompey fan. I felt Portsmouth was now my home and I had not seen West Ham regularly enough to warrant continued 'proper' support.

No one dare accuse me of being a fair weather fan though. My decision came when relegation was looming, the club were debt ridden and the squad thin. Malcolm Allison was in charge of Plymouth and we lost 5-1. Shortly afterwards we were relegated in bottom place to the fourth tier.

What had I done! In all honesty, nothing I regret. I just followed my heart and have never looked back. The time we spent in the old fourth division was among the best. Nick and I watched nearly every home game and a good number of away fixtures, including afternoon travel to some unappealing places like Newport County, Doncaster (on a winter's evening), and Wigan all the way by train.

Then, over twenty years on, an unexpected change in fortune. We won the Championship and went on to establish ourselves in the Premiership, winning the FA Cup in 2008 and reaching the final again in 2010. Wembley became our second home for two years.

Then it all went pear shaped, thanks to gross mismanagement and clueless owners. I expect that by May 2013 my life as a Pompey fan will have turned full circle and we may well be back in the bottom tier of English football.

Oh to be a footy fan!

How it was

A nostalgic look back to the golden era of football in modern times, the 60s and 70s, when men were men and boys idolised their heroes.

In my humble opinion it was English football's golden era, where 40 plus goals per week in the First Division was commonplace. No millionaire footballers in those days, they had a close affinity to the working and middle class men, women and children who went in their droves to matches.

Why the sixties and seventies and not the forties or fifties I hear the (even) older generation ask?

In my humble opinion (and reviews of vintage footage) the game started to change dramatically at the end of the 1950s in a number of ways that made it even more attractive.

Player equipment (balls and boots basically) went through a complete transformation. By the sixties, the players' skills began to take on a new dimension, developing towards the level of today.

I am certainly not saying there were not skillful players before the sixties, far from it. Looking at some of the footage of yesteryear I wonder how they were so skilful in those heavy boots, kicking around a lead balloon.

I believe that any decent player from that era would be as good their counterparts today with similar equipment and an equal opportunity to receive the same level of training, medical support and even psychology.

The skill levels of the sixties were still way behind the likes of Messi and Ronaldo today, but the lighter, more agile boots and modern ball definitely enabled a new kind of skill to develop.

Footballers in that era earned a very decent wage, but never became rich. After retirement, they had to find a normal job, if not lucky enough to remain in the game as a manager, coach or scout. They worked hard and fans came in their droves to watch these football greats, when tackles were hard and diving or rolling around on the ground was not tolerated.

If a player was 'hacked down', a common occurrence of the time, he would just wince, brush himself down and get on with it. But he would also make sure he took out revenge on the perpetrator at a convenient point, unless it was one of the true 'hard' men of the time.

I played football until the late nineties, but considered myself old school in that I never feigned injury for a foul or to gain advantage. I certainly did not know how to perform a dive, even if I had wanted to. However, by the late eighties I could see the early traits of (what I consider) cheating in this way from the younger generation of amateur players that were coming through.

Those Were the Days

Moore, Astle, Ball and Best,
Fan filled grounds, five hundred abreast;
Hunt, Greaves, Charlton and Law,
No fancy formations, goals galore.

They were honest and raw, no egos or riches;
Sublime skills on brown, mud soaked pitches;
No diving, no spitting, no peacock parade,
Just working class men plying their trade.

No tiaras or tantrums, no million pound fees,
Working a living with mud stained knees;
No time wasting antics, a game of two halves,
And true loyal fans, all waving their scarves.

Anfield, St. Andrews, Belle Vue and The Shay,
Three generations watching them play.
In all parts of England, from the South to the North,
Fans turned up in their millions to watch them go forth.

The sixties were special, a working man's sport,
Where hardly a game ended nought nought;
Just excitement and noise, with fans on a crest,
Those were the days, and simply the best.

Compared to some of my friends I was quite late in developing my passion for football. I assume that the main reason for this is that I did not have a lot exposure to the game. My father and older brothers were not avid supporters and did not attend matches, and the media coverage of football was low profile at the time.

I do remember playing some football from about the age of seven, joining in games in the school playground and occasionally kicking a ball about in the garden with my brothers. However, the garden kick-about never lasted long as the ball always ended up flying over the fence at the bottom of the garden within half an hour, where our grumpy neighbour put his garden fork through it before throwing it back.

I used to spend a lot of time with my best friend Steve and was often invited to tea at their house. Steve and I used to occasionally kick a ball around with other lads in the street, but more often than not we chose to play inside. I vividly remember his dad listening to the football results on the radio if I was there on a Saturday afternoon and being told to keep quiet if we were a bit verbal while they were being read out.

Steve's dad was a West Ham fan and he told me stories about when he used to live in the East End and go to games with his dad and uncle, seeing all of the great footballers of the time. I know he had been a few times since too. Over time, his stories sank in and I began to wonder what it would be like to go to a match. I wanted to see what it was like myself.

Just after the World Cup in 1966 and further stories of how he had seen Bobby Moore start his first game as a mere lad, I asked if I could go with him when he next went. He smiled and winked at me and said "You never know". I thought it unlikely until a few months later ...

First Match: The Build Up

A week before Christmas, no snow in the sky;
A cold and grey day, but I felt on a high.
The day following my birthday, the year sixty six,
My first football match, instead of the flicks.

I'd stayed over at Steve's house, my very best mate;
As a rare birthday treat, we'd stayed up quite late.
We'd been friends since the infants, way back in time;
His dad had to take us, as we were just nine.

A chip butty for lunch, then we left about one;
A few bob in my pocket and a bun from Steve's mum.
Steve's dad was a hammer fan, East End true,
A scarf round his neck, it was claret and blue.

By train and then bus, across London we went,
Past grey high-rise blocks, no red bricks and cement;
The "Bridge" was the venue, so not really a trek;
Anticipation ran through me, what should I expect?

It was a derby at Chelsea, an all London affair;
Approaching the ground, a buzz in the air.
Never seen so many vendors, on stalls and in vans,
Selling scarves, pendant badges, hot dogs and cans.

Reaching the turnstile, at the edge of the ground,
I felt slightly uneasy, seemed like millions around;
After tickets exchanged we squeezed through the gate,
Though not in control, I still felt quite safe.

Smelt burgers and onions sizzling away on a hob;
Steve's dad bought three programmes for under two bob;
We had seats high in the stand, to the West of the ground,
Climbed six flights of steps, but then easily found.

First Match: The Match

The teams came out to rapturous applause;
To me it was deafening, not even a pause.
It kicked off at three to loud manly cheers;
Steve's dad waved his scarf, some Chelsea fans jeered.

Looking down and around I was transfixed by the crowd,
So many thousands and ever so loud;
Narrow terrace walkways stood out like a groove,
Apart from some sways it seemed no one could move.

It was hard to believe seeing three World Cup greats;
Right there, so close, I'd have envious mates.
The game ebbed this way then that, never slow;
I watched in awe of the skills on show.

Goal after goal, there were five in each half;
The game was hypnotic, I was hooked from the start;
As the final whistle blew, it was hard to believe,
My first match had ended and we had to leave.

And so it had finished, a score draw, five all;
Hurst scored a hat-trick and was given the ball;
I guessed both teams were happy as no one had lost,
I knew nothing of points and what it might cost.

First Match: Post Match

We left the ground in a hurry, everyone was rushing;
Then we ran to the bus stop to avoid any crushing.
Went back to Steve's house for tea and ice cream,
My mind was still racing, it seemed like a dream.

I walked home at seven and felt like a man,
But more than that now, a real football fan.
But I needed to prove it, just to myself,
So decided to raid my big brother's shelf.
I wanted my heroes all over my wall;

Hurst, Peters, Moore all standing tall;
Four West Ham pics I'd eventually loot,
Nabbed from my brother's magazine "Shoot!"

Still very excited, I went off to bed,
With my new pin-up heroes above my head.
I dropped off thinking about the next game,
And if taken again, would it be just the same?

So that was back then, my very first game,
But Football has changed, it's now not the same;
Whilst not a West Ham fan now, the memories' not gone,
And I still have the programme, more than forty years on!

Popularity of the game in the 50s and 60s

While it is true that the largest crowds (and most ground record attendances) were seen in the 1930s and 1940s, football continued to enjoy a large spectator following throughout the 1950s and 1960s, with grounds in the top flights regularly filled to capacity.

The period from the 1920s to mid 1950s was a boom time for football across the United Kingdom. It was a working class sport affordable to everyone, including those who wanted to take their children. After the two World Wars the British population (in particular men) needed an affordable social outlet and football served this purpose well.

They didn't care how they packed the crowds in, if there was still a space to fill, it was. It was not an uncommon sight to see a fan who had fainted being passed down the terraces over the heads of those packed in so that they could be treated by the touchline for their ill effects.

Large standing only terraces outweighed the seating areas, where a dozen or so people stood for each person seated. Seats were for the gentry and few working class men could afford the extra shilling (5p) to utilise them.

Although terraces were generally a safe and cheap way to enjoy football, they would occasionally be proven dangerous. In the early days railway sleepers were commonly used to form a bank of gradually ascending viewing areas, but when wet they became slippery and as a result many fans suffered falls and broken bones.

They were soon replaced by concrete terracing at most grounds, but the common and dangerous practice of packing too many people into the ground became evident at Bolton Wanderers' Burnden Park in 1946.

It was estimated that more than 80,000 fans had entered the ground before they locked the gates. Many more who were locked out decided to climb a wall to gain entry. As they pushed forward into the ground the wall collapsed and hundreds of spectators were forced down a barrier-less section of the terrace under the weight of the crowd.

The game was eventually stopped when a police officer walked onto the pitch and towards the referee. He blew his whistle and pointed towards the motionless bodies lying at the edge of the pitch, stating "I believe those people over there are dead." Thirty-three people died and over 400 were injured in the disaster.

Of course there have been other well documented disasters in more modern times, including Ibrox in 1971, both Bradford and Heysel in 1985, and Britains' worst football disaster at Hillsborough in 1989. However, in those early days it is quite astonishing that more tragedies didn't occur when grounds were blatantly packed beyond safe numbers.

In the late 1950s ground and crowd safety did become a concern for the authorities. Although overcrowding restrictions were imposed, they were feebly enforced, and in the main ignored. In the early sixties, after further minor incidents due to over packed grounds, sensibility prevailed and clubs began to restrict excessive overcrowding.

To serve as a now and then comparison, the table on the following page lists English clubs who have crammed more than 50,000 fans into their ground and their current capacities today. A second table shows Scottish ground records and a selection of other clubs who still play in their original stadium and have historically managed to exceed their current ground capacity by two to three times. If you have visited some of these original grounds in the last ten years or so, you may wonder how they managed to squeeze all the fans in.

Club (Ground)	Record Attendance (Year)	Capacity in 2012[1]
Manchester City (Maine Road)	84,569 (1934)	47,405 (Etihad)
Manchester United (Old Trafford)	83,260 (1948)	75,811
Chelsea (Stamford Bridge)	82,905 (1935)	42,449
Everton (Goodison Park)	78,299 (1948)	40,157
Aston Villa (Villa Park)	76,588 (1946)	42,786
Sunderland (Roker Park)	75,118 (1933)	49,000 (St. of Light)
Spurs (White Hart Lane)	75,038 (1938)	36,230
Charlton Athletic (The Valley)	76,031 (1938)	27,111
Arsenal (Highbury)	73,295 (1946)	60,361 (Emirates)
Sheffield Weds (Hillsborough)	72,841 (1934)	39,812
Bolton (Burnden Park)	69,912 (1933)	28,100 (Reebok)
Newcastle (St James Park)	68,386 (1930)	52,409
Sheffield United (Bramall Lane)	68,287 (1936)	32,609
Huddersfield (Leeds Road)	67,037 (1932)	24,554 (Galpharm)
Birmingham City (St Andrews)	66,844 (1939)	29,409
West Brom (The Hawthorns)	64,815 (1937)	26,360
Blackburn Rovers (Ewood Park)	62,522 (1929)	31,154
Liverpool (Anfield)	61,905 (1952)	45,276
Wolves (Molineux)	61,315 (1939)	27,828
Cardiff City (Ninian Park)	57,893 (1953)	26,828 (Cardiff C St.)
Leeds United (Elland Road)	57,892 (1967)	37,900
Hull City (Boothferry Pak)	55,019 (1949)	25,404 (KC Stadium)
Burnley (Turf Moor)	54,775 (1924)	21,940
Middlesborough (Ayresome Park)	53,802 (1949)	34,998 (Riverside St.)
Crystal Palace (Selhurst Park)	51,482 (1979)	26,225

---

[1] Stadium names in brackets denote clubs who have moved from their original ground to a new stadium since the record attendance.

Coventry (Highfield Road)	51,455 (1967)	32,604 (Ricoh Arena)
Portsmouth (Fratton Park)	51,385 (1949)	21,178
Stoke City (Victoria Ground)	51,380 (1937)	27,740 (Britannia St.)

Table 1: Crowd attendance records of English clubs and grounds exceeding 50,000

Club (Ground)	Record Attendance (year)	Capacity in 2012
Rangers (Ibrox)	118,567 (1939)	51,082
Celtic (Celtic Park)	83,000 (1930)	60,832
Queen's Park (Hampden Park)	95,722 (1938)	52,103
Hibernian (Easter Road)	65,860 (1950)	17,500
Hearts (Tynecastle)	53,396 (1932)	17,420
Clyde (Shawfield)	52,000 (1908)	8,006 (B'wood)
Partick Thistle (Firhill)	49,838 (1922)	10,887
St. Mirren (Love Street)	47,438 (1949)	8,016 (St. Mirren P)
Aberdeen (Pittrodie)	45,061 (1954)	22,199
Dundee (Dens Park)	43,024 (1953)	12,085
Kilmarnock (Rugby Park)	35,995 (1962)	18,128
Motherwell (Fir Park)	31,306 (1952)	13,742
Raith Rovers (Stark's Park)	31,306 (1953)	10,104
Port Vale (Vale Park)	49,768 (1960)	19,148
Fulham (Craven Cottage)	49,355 (1938)	25,700
Oldham (Boundary Park)	47,671 (1930)	10,850
Notts County (Meadow Lane)	47,310 (1955)	20,280
Plymouth (Home Park)	43,984 (1936)	16,388
Bristol City (Ashton Gate)	43,335 (1935)	21,940
Preston NE (Deepdale)	42,684 (1938)	23,408
Barnsley (Oakwell)	40,255 (1936)	23,287
Brentford (Griffin Park)	39,626 (1938)	12,763
Blackpool (Bloomfield Road)	38,098 (1955)	16,007
Bury (Gigg Lane)	35,000 (1960)	11,313
Leyton Orient (Brisbane Road)	34,345 (1964)	9,311
Watford (Vicarage Road)	34,099 (1969)	17,477

Swindon Town (County Ground)	32,000 (1972)	14,983
Peterborough (London Road)	30,096 (1965)	14,793
Bournemouth (Dean Court)	28,799 (1957)	9,776
Rochdale (Spotland)	24,371 (1949)	10,149

Table 2: Crowd attendance records of Scottish and other selected Clubs

Passion United

Excuse the phrase,
But they **were** golden days
When any team could win;
Each season in contention
For the title and the tin.

No foreign owners
And their billions,
No corporate boxes,
Or plastic fans;
Just passion of the millions
With names like Bert and Stan.

The crowds were huge,
Packed in so tight,
They stood side by side,
No menace or fight.

We queued at the turnstiles
Jostling for position,
Banter a plenty
'til we gained admission.

No tickets required
Just cash in hand,
Clicked through the gate
To the terrace or stand.

We stood on the terraces,
Cheering aloud,
Waving our scarves
Clacking rattles proud.

Through a tinny loudspeaker
Came the news of the team,
On the back of the programme
We ticked off who were playing.

But the memories are fading,
It's a different scene now,
But to the fans of the past,
Let's all take a bow.

Media Coverage

Today's younger generation of football followers would find it difficult to conceive the low media profile of football in the early to mid 60s and before, despite it being such a popular spectator sport. Newspaper coverage was limited to the couple of "sports" pages at the back. There were no dedicated pullouts or sports sections and reports of most games confined to a few lines.

The lack of coverage was even more apparent on Television. There were no sports channels, no 24 hour channels, and no club channels. Football only enjoyed cameo TV appearances where highlights of important matches were captured on Newsreels (short black and white films) that were subsequently broadcasted on TV or at the cinema via Pathe News.

There was no regular football aired on the two only available networks, BBC and ITV, until Match of the Day was first broadcasted in 1964. Even then, it started off on BBC2 as a means to prepare for full television coverage of the World Cup in 1966.

Following the World Cup, MOTD was screened weekly, early on a Saturday evening. It started as a 35 minute programme and showed highlights of one selected match only, in a grainy black and white broadcast. That was it, apart from short clips shown on the news covering major games.

In 1967 ITV's "The Big Match" came on air, but only to London viewers on a Sunday afternoon. Again, this covered one match only, where predominantly, a London club was involved.

The internet and mobile phone were still some 30 some years away, so football news travelled slowly. Basically, we had to rely on the papers to see match reports and pictures, or subscribe to one of the few football magazines that carried articles, reports, and league tables; by the time the weekly journals came through our letter box they were already out of date!

Football costs

The admission price in the mid 1950s for a top flight match was at most two shillings, or 10p in today's money. This represents less than 2% of the then average salary of £5.50 per week. An FA Cup Final (standing) ticket in 1954 was 3'6d, about 18p. Even the very best seats at Wembley in 1954 were only ten shillings (50p).

If re-calculated against today's average UK salary (£22,500), the 2011 average ticket price of £42 works out at just under 10% of a week's income. If ticket prices had increased in line with inflation over the same period, the admission price would only be around £2.20.

By the mid sixties the price had increased to around six shillings (30p) for an adult, mainly due to the maximum player wage being abolished in 1961. By the mid seventies the admission cost had risen to around £1.20, still very cheap when compared to the ridiculously over inflated prices of today. In the last two decades ticket prices have spiralled, where the average admission price has risen by more than 1,000 per cent.

As an example, the cheapest ticket for a Manchester United game in 1989 was £3.50. By 2010, the lowest priced ticket was £28. If the admission price had increased in line with inflation during the same period, it would have cost £6.20. In the same period, a ticket to watch Liverpool rose from £4 to £45, an increase of 1,025 per cent.

Of course there are major factors that contribute to the higher prices of today, such as the cost of re-building and running our modern stadia, and not least, the exorbitant transfer fees and players wages.

In stark contrast to my first match back in 1966, Sam, aged 10, attended his first match in April 2012. In 1966 it was probably no more than seven shillings (35p) for an adult and three shillings (15p) for a child. When Sam attended his first match at White Hart Lane, his dad had to shell out £53 for each ticket; there was no junior concession.

Sam went with his dad, older brother (16), his friend Callum (10), and Callum's dad. For two adults and three boys, the total admission cost alone was a staggering £285 (including a £20 booking fee). In 1966, to take the same contingent would have cost no more than £1.15.

If you take into account the cost today of three programmes, a couple of scarves, food and drink, travel and parking, the total cost for the day at Spurs would have been approaching £400!

Sam's mum and dad are close friends of mine, and after talking to Sam about his experience I thought it would be a good idea to write about it. Even though it seems out of context chronologically, I wanted to include it here to serve as a direct comparison to the way I saw things at my first match.

Kids of today are probably more worldly-wise and less naïve than their counterparts of forty years ago. Their outlook is different because the world is so different and they probably view things from a different perspective. They have grown up with mass media coverage of the game where football can be consumed 24 by 7 in some form or another.

But then maybe this isn't true of the basic experience as a whole, like the raw experience of seeing and hearing a large crowd, or being so close to their heroes, seeing them in the flesh for the first time.

I was keen to capture Sam's thoughts and the visions he encapsulated that day, and how they compared to mine. I spent more than an hour talking to Sam, gathering his thoughts and memories about his big day out.

The following is my interpretation of those thoughts, written as free form prose as it seemed a more appropriate manner to tell the story in his way.

Sam's First Match

Excitement dawned early on that day.
April 29th at last he thought.
Once it was weeks away
But now so suddenly here;
His very first match.

Would it become a ritual later in life?

To Sam a unique birthday treat, who
At just ten, was now following the path
Of millions of ten year olds before him;
Following in his father's footsteps
All those years ago.

The morning came quickly;
Up quite early, he watched some TV.
He was excited and wished it was time to leave;
But time went so slow, slower than he had ever known.
Ten past Nine. Look again, still ten past nine;
The seconds turned into minutes, minutes into hours;
Or seemingly so.
Would 11 ever come?
But it did; they were ready to go.

Grandad called as they were about to leave,
To wish him luck he said.
Did Sam need luck?
I don't think so; he really meant the team;
Sam was a third generation follower.

Then they left.
Sam, his Dad and brother Ollie.
His friend Callum went too,
With his dad, both followers alike.
Picked them up Just around the corner.

In reality a two hour trip, but
More time was needed,
To avoid motorway madness,
And allow for the London mayhem,
Where everyone crosses each other
To get from a to b, and sometimes c.

On the M25 they were stuck,
He could have walked faster.
A snail could.

He then spotted something strange
And rather funny;
He laughed and pointed out to everyone
The car next to them, where a ladies dress
Was part hanging outside of the door;
The grownups laughed, Oliver smiled;
Sam and Callum giggled for ages at the sight.

The plan was right; they crawled through London,
Bumper to bumper.
What time was it now?
Only 12.30, but time must have stopped;
It seemed like hours ago they left.

PASSION UNITED

Through London they went,
Street after street meandered;
Light after light they stopped;
London so dirty, so much litter;
Where was the dazzle, the large shops, the glitter?
It was like Sam's small home town;
Only fifty of them in a row.

They turned right at some lights;
He could just make out the ground ahead.
A mass of people appeared; from nowhere;
So many fans, so many scarves,
So many stalls selling them.
Massive burger vans;
Not like the one in the market,
But big silver, red and golden ones,
Bright lights adorning them.

They parked and joined the throng.
Careful not to lose sight of Dad or the others
He kept close though not really scared.
They bought chips and ate them walking along
With 100s of other chip, hot dog and burger eaters;
No wonder they had big burger vans.

Suddenly it loomed large, larger than life;
White Hart Lane.
When chips were finished they went into
The Spurs "mega-store".
He thought, it isn't really a mega-store,
Not like B&Q or Sainsburys.
It is a shop, no bigger than our Tesco Express.

But he now had a Spurs shirt and a scarf;
He felt like the rest around him and would now
Be recognised as one of them.
He felt proud and part.

Into the ground they headed;
Thousands at a time going through the tiny entrances
Carved out of the side of the massive stadium.
They climbed flight after flight;
Voices and cheering were echoing loud
From below and above.

Then they were there;
The colour, the noise resounding
As they walked into the inner sanctum,
This was it; he felt he was really there now.

In their seats it was so different from TV;
More real than even their big plasma screen.
The pitch looked so close and ever so green;
The players were out training
They were larger, clearer than he'd ever seen.

As the players walked off, the team was announced;
No Pienaar, no Parker and no Defoe;
In Sandro and Rose,
Two players he didn't even know.

Suddenly, as if from nowhere,
the Star Wars theme blazed out;
"Come on you Spurs" rang around
In a communal shout
From all sides of the ground.

Spurs had all the play;
His dad said they were dominating.
This seemed true to him.
Whenever Blackburn had it,
Spurs won it back then attacked again.

In minute twenty two it happened,
Spurs scored! van der Vaart,
And although not clear to him how,
The ball seemed to go in, then straight out.
But everyone was screaming and cheering
There was a delay for a decision; it was given,
More cheers!

He thought it was amazing!
The cheering went on and on.
He'd never heard anything so loud
Or for so long.
He stood up, sat down, then up again;
Back down again, then up;
He had to, everyone else was doing it.

Spurs kept attacking,
Raid after raid on the Blackburn goal;
Every time Spurs came close they all stood up,
He knew it was the natural thing to do.

Then half time came.
Dad bought him a curry pie
Which he quickly ate.
Ollie teased him about having curry breath.
Dad told Ollie to stop it
Or he would tell everyone around them
He supported Chelsea; which he did.
Sam and Callum laughed at this,
They then pointed at Ollie, quietly saying
"Chelsea fan, Chelsea fan".

The second half was like the first;
Spurs still "dominating"
Blackburn hardly having the ball.
Then Walker scored, a screamer from a free kick
He went through the same ritual of
Standing up and cheering loudly.

On the big screen
The attendance was given; 35,987
He thought, only thirteen didn't turn up.
The match finished in all of a sudden.
It went so much quicker than watching on TV.

As they left the stadium
He wondered how it was possible that
So many people can get out so quickly,
Filling the street
That was empty minutes before.

On the way home they drove
Close by two other stadiums,
Wembley and Twickenham;
Though from a distance only
They still seemed so large;
He wondered how much bigger
And nosier they could be than White Hart Lane.

It seemed a long journey home,
Outside it was grey and cold.
As rain started to fall
His mind drifted around
To thoughts of Spurs and football.

He will always remember his first match.
The occasion;
How the morning stopped,
But the day flew by.
Seeing his team and the players so close,
Being amongst so many people;
But especially the noise; he could still hear it.

Dedicated to Sam, son of my good friends Darren and Anna.

The 70s

During mid to late summer 1969 my parents started to view country properties, mainly in Hampshire. They wanted to move out of Brixton (where I was born) to lead a more rural way of life.

By December they had an offer accepted on an old Colonial style bungalow in the outer reaches of a parish called Ropley. We moved on January 2nd 1970. I was allowed to travel down with the removal men, the first time I had ever been in a lorry!

Being just twelve, I was quite excited at the prospect of this new life. The garden was huge, just over two acres, with maybe ten wooden sheds of various sizes dotted amongst an old orchard and very overgrown garden. I could play on our land or venture into the thick woods at the back. There was an abundance of wild life I had never witnessed, including foxes, pheasants, badgers, big noisy crickets ... and slow worms! I actually thought these were baby snakes when I first discovered one under a sheet of corrugated iron not far from the bungalow.

I had never seen a snake before, apart from at a zoo. When I was younger my Nan had a shop in East Molesey. In the garden was a disused, rusting milk delivery van. When we visited we often played in it, but she never liked it, telling us to leave it alone and warning us there were probably snakes in the long undergrowth underneath it. This fascinated me and when not being watched I would gingerly look underneath it, poking into the long grass with a longish stick in the hope of seeing one. But I never did and they remained a mystery to me until I discovered the slow worms. When I first saw one I ran back to the house yelling that I had found a snake.

Despite my excitement at this new way of life, when making that final journey out of London in the removal van, a couple of things occurred to me that made me feel slightly uneasy.

Although it seems silly now and these initial thoughts were quickly proved to be totally unfounded, I actually wondered if they knew about football in this remote part of Hampshire, or whether we would be able to listen to the radio, or even watch television. On our previous excursions to Hampshire and beyond to view various properties, I never remembered seeing any football pitches or goalposts.

I started to imagine that this countryside was akin to darkest Africa where modern life had not yet reached. I asked the removal man in the seat next to me; he laughed out loud repeating my question to the driver, who laughed too. Although I knew they found it funny that I should think that, I still wasn't sure!

Once settled in, I soon discovered we were not in deepest Africa and I started to wonder when I might play football again or go to a match.

I went to a few games at Southampton with a school friend and his dad, the highlight being when the mighty Manchester United came to town, thrashing Southampton 5-2. The likes of Best, Charlton, Law and Kidd played that day, heroes I had tried to emulate in the playground with a tennis ball, or on the school playing fields at lunchtime in fine weather. However, I must stress I was not a Southampton fan! They were the nearest club to us and were in the first division.

With the advent of skinheads in the late 60s, came an increasing air of menace; football hooliganism. This became uncomfortably apparent after the Man United v Southampton game, when fans went on the rampage in the city after the match. A darker side to football had emerged.

I still had relatives in London. My auntie and uncle lived in Catford and I had a good relationship with my cousin Chris, a year younger. We used to visit them frequently and I would sometimes stay over. We often went to football matches, first with big cousin Brian, but shortly after on our own after proving ourselves as street wise.

My cousins supported Crystal Palace. Chris and I went to watch Palace at Orient one Saturday afternoon, around 1972. Two nerve racking things happened that day related to hooliganism.

Firstly, when at the match, we inadvertently found ourselves on the edge of the Palace fans close to the Orient fans, basically in "no mans land" on the terrace. A few police officers were liberally stewarding and the two sets of fans were probably no more than 20 feet apart.

During the second half the chanting between the two sets of fans became louder, and more menacing. Some older Palace fans beside us started to swear loudly over us towards the Orient fans, making typical gestures and egging them on to come and join them.

I remember a man standing beside me, probably in his twenties, saying to me "Are you ready for a rush boy?" I was not really sure what he meant, but it didn't sound appealing.

Suddenly, with no time to react both sets of fans rushed at each other; Chris and I, still at the edge, were sandwiched between them. I can't remember exactly what happened but I know we were pushed forward as the fans engaged, I just kicked out aimlessly as fists and feet started flying.

I quickly grabbed Chris and we managed to sort of crouch down and somehow manoeuvre back between the mass of Palace fans and away from the frontline.

It only lasted about 20 seconds as the Police quickly converged to restore order. However, it scared me so much that I was shaking and can't remember what happened in the game after that, we were more concerned in finding a safe place to stand until we were let out. We learnt a valuable lesson that day in where not to stand at a football match!

Then, on the way home, something even more sinister happened. We had to take the tube from Leytonstone to Waterloo, before taking an over ground train home to Catford Bridge. The tube train stopped at Mile End. West Ham were playing at home that day. A group of West Ham skinheads jumped into the carriage we were sat in, via the end doors furthest from us.

My heart stopped as they mindlessly started to hit out at people on the train, including a woman. We were stiff with panic. Chris was hurriedly trying to hide his Palace scarf under his jacket. I thought "but I support West Ham and am now going to be beaten up by them if they spot us".

Luckily, the train doors beeped; it was about to set off. They jumped off as fast as they had jumped on. We were saved by the beep!

To this day I honestly think that if we had been seated further down the carriage, or were spotted by them earlier, or had the train stayed at the station for 20 seconds more, we would both have been badly hurt, possibly maimed. It was the worst experience of my life as a football fan.

All I could think about in those 30 seconds we were at the station was how I would try to plea that I was actually a West Ham fan and had just gone to watch Palace with my cousin because I was not able to get a West Ham ticket. It was a truly scary experience, caused by mindless thugs.

The Darker Side

In local pubs and working men's clubs,
In cities and towns up and down the land;
Amateur generals gather and scheme;
An away day needs to be planned.

They're not down and outs or short of cash,
Wearing designer clothes and Burberry hats.
Though attached to a team, support is hollow,
Caring more for the battle, than who they follow.

When match day arrives
The clans assemble;
The tension mounts
Making innocents tremble.

Ringleaders orchestrate
Like modern day Neroes,
Their young armies in waiting,
Sucking up to their heroes.

It was a dark time for football,
Of men mindless and violent;
Though firms still exist,
They are now mainly silent.

Twats

At every match you get them.

The one with his brat
And his Burberry hat;
The over aged skins
With their double chins,
Still bald as coots,
In their Levi jeans
And designer boots;
The old man half deaf
Hurling abuse at the ref;
Young lads so canned
They can hardly stand;
Then the geezer behind
Who seems out of his mind;
And the twat in front
With an opinion so blunt
And who acts like a...

Fan Passion

If you are a football fan, I hope that this section and the subsequent poems will stir your thoughts and memories. I have taken a (sometimes sideways) look at how some fans see the game and how they react to certain situations or events. Some will almost certainly remind you of fans you have come across on your travels. Some you may know, some you may recognise by the character.

I have mixed with thousands of fans from clubs up and down the land. I have also shared discussions and opinions with hundreds of individuals from all walks of life; in pubs, on coaches and trains, queueing at the turnstiles, and even brief exchanges at the urinals. Some have become match day friends; some you may talk to or banter with, even if you wouldn't spend an evening with them by choice.

But we all have one thing in common. We share a passion.

We may follow different teams and react in various ways to different outcomes, but we all display passion in one form or another. Over the years I have seen a diverse spectrum of passion and how it subsequently affects our emotions.

I have vivid memories of the two scales of passion when we played at West Brom, in 2002, the year before we won the championship. It was a very cold day in late February. I went with my daughter Vicky (aged 21) and long term friend Nick. For some reason Vicky only took a light jacket, which I hadn't noticed, wearing just a tee shirt under her Pompey shirt.

West Brom were going for promotion (which they subsequently achieved as runners up to Man City). They also duly thumped us 5-0. At half time and four down, Vicky was frozen. I gave up my winter coat to her, leaving me very cold, but not as frozen as she had become. As I queued to buy some much needed hot Bovril, I knew it would seem a long second half!

The second half continued in the same vein as the first, West Brom totally dominating, our boys totally lacklustre. With about fifteen minutes to go West Brom attacked yet again and scored their fifth. I looked around the stadium as the players celebrated.

The Baggies in the section to our right were jumping up and down, some in no more than a football top, looking deliriously happy and not cold at all. I was beginning to shiver, which added to my annoyance of having to listen to their "Boing Boing Baggies" chants.

Just below me a young Pompey fan of no more than nine was crying and being consoled by his dad. Another lad about five seats along to their left, in his early twenties I guessed, had his head in his hands, shaking it slowly from side to side every few seconds or so.

I looked at Vicky next to me. She was still frozen and had a look of disgust on her face, a look I had not recognised since she was about eight and had tripped over onto a pile of dog muck whilst kicking a ball about in our local park.

She looked back at me and remarked that she would never go and watch this pile of crap again. Nick just sat there with an air of resignation, depicting a look that he had been there before, many, many times.

I looked back to the pitch, West Brom were attacking again... they narrowly missed going six up and the Baggies' fans started up again, with choruses of "We're going up" and "Can we play you every week?"

Vicky had now slumped completely into her seat, nearly disappearing through the crack it seemed, huddled in a ball with my large coat wrapped tightly around her.

We were truly rubbish that day; we never even won a corner.

Vicky didn't actually carry out her threat and continued to watch the Blues; the ritual carried on. Just over a year later, in April 2003, we went to watch Pompey play at Walsall. If we won we would go top again and almost ensure promotion. We did both.

I saw a different sort of passion from Vicky and the jubilant Portsmouth fans around me that day.

Saturday Ritual

It's just a Saturday ritual my dear.
So have no fear
And let's be clear,
I'm not gallivanting,
I've no bird in tow,
Think of it more
Like I'm off to a show;
I'll be back before you know.

And yes the pub is also part
Of the ritual we must trek,
But please take heart
As I never really notice,
The barmaids so buxom
And breasts so pink;
I never ever touch them,
I just order the drink.

And when we lose,
I'm sorry if I swear;
It's like when the junior stylist
Fucks up your lovely hair.
And that time I kicked the cat
I swear it was not meant,
But still you banished me that night,
To the garden and the tent.

Image "The Wheatsheaf, Altrincham" © Copyright Matthew Wilkinson

And you know I can't go shopping,
We tried that once before;
The jab with your brolly hurt so much
When I tried to see the score;
And you know you can't come with me,
Last time you caught the flu,
Your hands were blue, your face like ice
As the final whistle blew.

So help me with this ritual,
Its generations old;
Just spare a thought for us poor souls
As we shiver in the cold.

Dedicated to the "footy widows".

Rose Tinted Glasses

Oh I wish I had a pair
Of those rose tinted glasses,
Then I wouldn't really care
How we lost to those smartarses.

Tony has an old pair,
They serve him very well,
Cos when we lose it's never fair
And not our fault we fell.

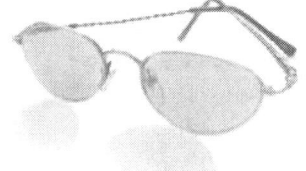

We're sublime when we win,
They're so lucky if we draw,
But if we lose he'll use his spin
And clutch at any straw.

"You must have seen that handball …
We all saw it from our section,
The stupid ref didn't make the call,
Didn't look in that direction"

If we lose again this Saturday,
He can always blame the ref,
Or the other teams foul play,
Or the keeper being deaf.

The next time I see Tony,
I'm going to ask for his optician;
Though it may be just baloney
It will help my disposition.

And while it may not stop us losing
Or stop me getting fraught,
I'll have a reason of my choosing
As to why it's not our fault.

So I need to have a pair
Of those rose tinted glasses,
So when we lose, we can share
How decisions turned to farces.

We all know one. Dedicated to my good friend Tony, who by his own admission owns a pair.

Jim

He loves it when they win;
With face beaming bright
He pumps the air;
With an infectious grin,
Shouts "get in there".

But when they lose
It's a very different story,
Like nothing worse could happen.
The red mist descends,
His tone transcends,
It really does his head in.

When he watches on TV
And the other team's just scored,
As his hopes turn to fears,
His chin hits the floor,
He'll be close to tears;
No more hearty cheers.

He'll then shout and curse
And sometimes worse;
He's like the Hulk
And throws a sulk;
Won't even talk,
Then takes a walk;
A private mourning
Without warning.

From the pram go his toys,
Shouts at his boys,
Then his face turns red,
As he drops his head,
Like it's made of lead.

But it's early doors
His team now scores;
He's ok again.
With barely a twitch,
Like a flick of a switch,
Goes from mad to sane.

I'm not such a rash soul,
And take the game as a whole;
But there are plenty like him,
That I bet you all know;
An emotional "Jim"

Dedicated to Jim, a friend and Southampton fan. He is the most animated fan I know, especially when things are not going their way!

Decisions, Decisions

The man in black, the man in the middle, however you refer to them, referees are a fundamental part of the game, but they can be as frustrating to fans as your own team when they are playing like donkeys.

Without the referee, football couldn't exist as a formal sport. I can't think of a competitive team sport which doesn't require a referee, umpire, judges, or equivalent. The one exception is amateur golf, where you and your fellow players are the effective referees.

I once heard referees referred to as "Marmite" men, not because they traditionally wear black, but because you can either love 'em or hate 'em, depending on their performance. Though I suspect love is a bit of a strong word to use, it's more a case of respecting them when they have a good game. I can't ever remember anyone at a match saying "Oh, it's *so-and-so*, I love him".

When I played football I generally had a good relationship with referees. At an amateur level I actually appreciated the fact that they gave up their Saturday afternoon or Sunday morning for next to nothing, for the love of the game, where they were often abused and occasionally even threatened.

I was only sent off twice. The first time was slightly bizarre and I remember the situation well. I knew the referee and I also knew he was very fickle too, and reminded the team of this before we left the changing rooms.

The match was being played in a good spirit with no major incidents. About mid way through the second half, with the score at 1-1, the opposition put a ball into our box and our normally sturdy centre half misjudged the bounce, but he somewhat recovered to stoop down and awkwardly chest it away from the pursuing forward. The referees' whistle blew and he was running into the box pointing at the spot.

We were all bewildered. I was tracking back into the box at the time and was just behind the referee when he blew up for the penalty; I was the first to question his decision.

I simply asked him why he had given the penalty. He immediately responded "Handball. You're defender handled the ball". I responded "No way ref, he chested it away". He replied "No he didn't, he clearly handled the ball". I again protested, but he just shook his head. As I started to walk away I said "Jesus".

The referee then shouted out "Number eight, come here". I turned around and walked the couple of yards back to him with my hands on my hips (it seems an instinctive thing to do when you are in trouble with the referee). I thought he was simply going to warn me not to question his decisions, but he took out his notebook and asked for my name. I said "You are not you going to book me are you?" He replied "No, I am sending you off".

I was stunned. I naturally asked "Why?" He immediately responded "You swore at me. It is a sending off offence to swear at an official"

I immediately protested my innocence at his accusation stating "No I didn't, what did I say?" He replied "Yes you did, you blasphemed as you walked away"

At this point I simply laughed and stated "You are joking ref!" But he wasn't and I had to leave the field. I was fuming but turned to watch the ensuing penalty. Their centre forward scuffed his kick and our keeper easily saved it. Some justice I thought, as I slowly trudged back towards the changing rooms.

After a short shower and changing, I watched the remaining 10 minutes from the sideline. We held on and the match ended 1-1. This at least put me in a better frame of mind.

As the referee left the field, I said "Roy, since when has what I said been a swear word? Or is blasphemy included in the rule book as a sending off offence?" I wasn't aggressive but felt frustrated and wanted a valid reason for his decision as I was sure "Jesus" (as an exclamation) could not be considered a sending off offence.

He looked slightly uneasy at my question but ignored me anyway, looking down as he walked briskly towards the changing rooms. I had a quick chat with some of the lads about it who agreed it was the strangest sending off they had witnessed. I left them to shower and change and went home.

That evening, our manager called me to say that Roy came into our changing room after the match and had told him he was quite religious and that my remark had upset him. However, he said he would not formally report it and I escaped a fine or ban.

I personally think that Roy had retrospectively felt foolish after the match and was not prepared to put the true reason for sending me off into his report.

MIB

They annoy us,
They frustrate us,
They can even make us scream,
And you'd think by some decisions
They're paid by the other team.

They're blind at will
And deaf as well,
It seems they rarely get it right;
When a single poor misjudgement
Can send us to our plight.

They're whistle happy
And brandish cards
Like they're going out of fashion.
They've surely never played the game
And have no idea of passion.

But joking apart, it's a serious affair,
They're not really one of us;
Men In Black harbour aliens,
In humans they don't care.

*Dedicated to the men in black... or
green, yellow and even pink nowadays!*

Top Image "Confirmation?" © Copyright Matthew Wilkinson

The International Stage of Football

The first recognised international football match took place way in 1872, fifty years before the World Cup was even conceived, when Scotland and England played a challenge match in Glasgow that ended goalless.

The first tournament played at international level was our own British Home Championships in 1884. Due to the rise in popularity of football globally by the turn of the century, football appeared at the 1900 and 1904 Summer Olympics as a demonstration sport, but it was restricted to an amateur level and no medals were awarded.

FIFA was founded in 1904, and they staged a low key tournament in 1908, but no formal professional level intercontinental tournaments took place until the first World Cup in 1930.

At the 1908 Olympics in London, football became an official competition. The Football Association planned the event, but again it was an amateur event only. FIFA took responsibility for managing the 1914 Olympic football tournament, describing the event as a "World Football Championship" for amateurs.

This effectively paved the way for the 1920 Olympics to become the first intercontinental football competition. FIFA also organised the next two Olympic football tournaments in 1924 and 1928. In 1924 FIFA started to plan the first professional international tournament.

The first World Cup tournament was formally conceived in 1928 and took place in 1930 in Uruguay, with the hosts winning the tournament.

There was no qualification (the only time ever) and thirteen countries took part.

The Football Association had fallen out with FIFA some years before and attending the inaugural World Cup was not even considered by the home nations. Leading up to the tournament, no European countries had entered by the closing date. To reach South America, it was a costly and time consuming three week journey by boat. However, after pressure from FIFA, four European teams eventually entered, being Belgium, France, Romania and Yugoslavia.

When it kicked off there were four groups, one of four and three of three. The group winner went straight into the semi-final. Amongst the four seeded teams was the USA, who won their qualifying group, but they were subsequently thrashed 6-1 by Argentina. Incidentally, Uruguay won by the same score against Yugoslavia in the other semi-final. Uruguay beat Argentina 4-2 in the final.

None of the home nations played in the World Cup tournaments until 1950. England and Scotland both qualified after the Home International championships were used as the qualification criteria. However, Scotland subsequently withdrew due to the stubbornness of the Scottish FA insisting that they would only go as Home International championship winners, but they finished runners up to England.

Oh how I would love to see the World Cup staged in Britain again. And if we were to have a shared British tournament, how exciting would it be to see all of our home nations competing as joint host nations.

Alas, 2018 wasn't to be. It seems that politics, lies, backstabbing and possibly corruption put paid to our failed bid.

Eng-er-land!

Supporting England is frustrating. They are an enigma to me. Without doubt, we have one of the most loyal and passionate set of supporters, even if not the most colourful, but we go through tournament hell time after time.

I am writing this section just ten days after England lost against Italy in the quarter finals of the Euros 2012.

Yet again, we couldn't hold our nerve in a penalty shoot out. However, I think we were lucky to progress that far in the match anyway. Italy simply outplayed us; we had a fifteen minute spell in the first half when we put them on the back foot, but over the duration of ninety minutes they were too clever for us and always looked more comfortable on the ball.

In major competitions why can't we compete with and occasionally turn over the top sides? By these I mean Argentina, Brazil, France, Holland, Italy, Portugal, Spain, and of course Germany.

France are currently fourteenth in the World rankings, while England are sixth. Yet, despite taking the lead in the Group match, we laboured against them after our goal, letting them back in to equalise.

The fact is that we have not won a competitive (non friendly) game against any of the world's top eight for ten years, when we beat Argentina 1-0 in the 2002 World Cup finals in Japan. Even then it was via a penalty. We have to go back to September 2001 when we outplayed a top side, thrashing Germany 5-1 in Munich.

I am no football coach or expert, but I have watched enough football at the top level (both league and International) to spot what the key differences are between our style of play and the top teams.

In my opinion, our style of play has gone backwards over the last ten years. We seem less comfortable on the ball than we were in the nineties and early noughties. Meanwhile, the top sides have improved their skill levels and take a completely different approach to the way they play. They zip the ball around with ease; when a good player receives the ball he always has options and in a single flowing move makes the pass that puts the opposition on the back foot.

We, too often, seem to need to fully control the ball, before looking at our options and making a decision. This gives the opposition time to close us down quicker, putting additional pressure on the player, and far too often the ball goes backwards or is lost.

Yet we are capable of creating flowing moves. We showed spells against France, Sweden and Italy that we can move the ball up the field swiftly and create chances. I am convinced that our players are as skillful on an individual basis as our continental and South American counterparts, but we do not seem to be able to play on the same level. It seems to me that this is not our instinctive style of play and it only happens in short bursts throughout the duration of a match. We fail to be able to dominate long spells of a match, even against mediocre sides. So Maybe it is the coaching style?

Ok, bitch over!

I am turning my attention to the good times, when England were a dominant force in World football. Before that, here is a poem I wrote ahead of the Euros 2012 finals.

England's Euro (Dream?)

Success so long ago
Since kings in sixty six;
Now we're up for it again
And need this like a fix.

The nation needs a lift right now,
The timing can't be better;
So come on lads, do your best
To release our football fetter.

Like heroes at Dunkirk,
Go forward England's best,
Be lions of the realm
And go beyond the test.

Put complacency to one side,
No flattering with deception,
We need to take it to them,
And destroy our old perception.

I know we have the talent,
Our league is far the best,
But we need to live the challenge
To lay the ghosts to rest.

Every fan out there with you,
And the millions here back home,
Will be with you all the way
With each attack you play.

Make us proud against the frogs,
Then simply mash the Swedes,
Make the pubs rock and roar,
Make us wild when you score.

Show them you have passion,
We're better than them by miles,
Hustle, hassle... even kick a bit,
Like Ball and Nobby Stiles.

Show them that we're up for it,
It's now time to perform.
Three Ukraine wins, finish top,
Then the Euros we can storm.

Post Note

Alas, it wasn't to be. For the first time I have ever known, most England fans I talked to before the tournament thought England would struggle to even qualify from their group. As it turned out we won the group; suddenly our expectations and optimism rose; yes, of course we can beat the Italians, why not?

Well, as previously documented, we are not at their level. Our quest to release our 1966 ball and chain goes on.

Sixty Six

After three score and six,
Football finally came home,
They gathered in England,
Spain and Germany scorn.

No qualifying was needed
For our lions in white,
Wembley was ready
For our boys to excite,
The stage was set,
For the world's elite.

Even before they kicked off,
The cup went astray,
But Jules Rimet was found
Hidden under some bushes,
Thank god for Pickles;
Who saved English blushes!

No African nations,
They were out from the start;
FIFA upset them,
They declined to take part

Two wins and a draw
And no goals conceded,
We eased through the group
And into the quarters.

A tough game in prospect
With kickers united;
Though bodies were bruised
Our confidence not dented.
Then Rattin walked
And victory was scented;
Hurst then struck late
Argentina were baulked.

The semi was close,
Eusebio shone bright;
But two up we went,
We were winning the fight.
With eight minutes to go
The black panther struck,
We played tight and held on,
Our dream still intact.

At the end of July
On a warm summer's day,
English and Germans
Walked side by side
Down Wembley Way.

Into Wembley they poured,
The tension was mounting.
On our fine men in white
The nation were counting.

The flags fluttered proudly
Above the cauldron of noise,
When they came on the pitch
Cheers rang loud for our boys.

Our toughest test yet,
The game ebbed each way,
Then the blonde German struck
Following excellent play.

But the lead was short lived;
A free kick from Moore;
A fine header dispatched
And Hurst's first drew us level.

There were plenty of chances
As the half went by,
But we looked the stronger
As the first half expired.

The second was tighter
With both teams playing wary,
Chances did come
But lines always cleared,
Both teams holding strong
No real cracks appeared.

Towards the end
England were pushing;
And with twelve minutes to go,
The Germans received
A second Hammer blow;
GOAL! For England,
Now Peters the hero.

We just had to hang on
Then the crown would be ours,
The Germans kept coming
Their fans started to rouse.

Just two minutes to go,
German hopes nearly dead,
Another cross reigns in,
Charlton clears with his head.

As the clock ticks down
A free kick against us;
Hit into our box
Only partially cleared...
Then something unspoken,
Weber poaches;
English hearts broken.

Extra time beckoned
When the Swiss whistle blew;
It was certainly a game
And still not yet through.

Just a short break to ponder,
We looked a bit rocky,
Faces slightly forlorn,
The Germans more cocky.

Extra time underway,
The game opened up,
Though legs started to tire,
We still had some fight,
When a historical moment
Set Wembley alight.

Hurst turned and shot,
It hit the bottom of the bar,
Then crashed down on the line;
But did it cross? A decision ajar.

English arms went up;
Controversy reigned,
Everyone looked to the line,
Awaiting the decision
The outcome was kind,
It was Swiss precision;

With minutes to go
We were still leading;
We'd been here before,
Knew we had to dig deep,
And ideally get four.

Less than a minute to go,
One last German attack,
It breaks down yet again,
As Moore sweeps it up field
And Hurst bursts clear like a train.

No German resistance
As he runs towards goal;
Just the keeper to beat,
He hurls in a shot,
A final Hammer blow
As it flies in the net.

England's finest moment,
We were now the elite;
The tough Germans broken,
We'd pulled off the feat.

Stairs climbed, cup collected,
Then proudly held high,
The crowd in raptures;
The sun shone in the sky.

Moore held aloft
As the cup was paraded;
They moved round the ground,
Boys still looking big,
Their faces beamed bright
As Nobby danced his jig.

Dedicated to our '66 heroes and to the memories of Sir Alf Ramsey, Bobby Moore and Alan Ball.

Football's Greatest

As you have probably gathered, I am a football romantic. Although I still love the game in its current form today, like a classic black and white movie, I find the memories of the past greats irresistible.

In my younger years as a schoolboy football nut there were plenty of heroes that I watched in awe, trying to emulate their skills in the parks, playgrounds and streets. Not just British players, but world greats like Alberto, Muller, Rivelino, Beckenbauer, Eusébio, Cruyff, and of course, Pelé. Even before my time, boys before me had heroes in the 40s and 50s like Di Stefano, Puskas, Garincha and Yashin.

The only downside is something I previously alluded to, in that the media coverage of the game in that era was low key, and footage of the greats scant. Compared to today, when just about every game and kick is televised, the vast majority of the skills displayed by these great players has been lost to the memory of the fans who were lucky enough to be there on the day.

For interest and to demonstrate this, I conducted some basic research. I put the following searches into You Tube for video clips showing Alfredo Di Stéfano, Ferenc Puskás, Bobby Charlton, Eusébio, Gerd Müller, Johan Cruyff, Diego Maradona, Zinedine Zidane and Lionel Messi. These players represent some of the greats covering seven decades.

Although not scientifically conclusive, the number of hits found for each player speaks for itself.

Player	No. of hits
Alfredo di Stéfano (1940s)	2,530
Ferenc Puskás (1950s)	2,040
Bobby Charlton	1,500
Eusébio (1960s)	11,600
Gerd Müller (1960s/70s)	5,450
Johan Cruyff (1970s)	3,960
Diego Maradona (1980s)	34,300
Zinedine Zidane (1990s)	23,100
Lionel Messi (present day)	86,800

I found the number of hits displayed for Eusébio surprising. My assumption is that either a lot of Portuguese fans have uploaded repeat clips, or filming football in Portugal was more prevalent than anywhere else!

Incidentally, I also searched on Cristiano Ronaldo, which resulted in a massive 369,000! On closer inspection, I found that plenty of other "Ronaldos" appeared in the listing, not just Cristiano.

Being British, we were blessed with great players too. Finney, Lofthouse, Edwards, Law, Moore, Charlton, Charles, Greaves, MacKay, Haynes, Lennox, Banks, and of course, Best.

We will all have our opinions and favourites, be it the legends of the past, or present day icons. So who is the greatest player of them all?

I think it depends what qualities you consider are the best to determine "the greatest". Inevitably the names bandied about the most are midfielders or forwards, simply because they have a greater impact in a match, or greater chance of being match winners.

Maybe it would be fairer to judge and have various categories of the greats, based on their positions rather than how many they score, or how they dribble and ghost past players. The most common names put forward are Pelé, Maradona and Messi (even though Messi is only half way through his career!).

In my eyes, sticking to the match winner theme that is centric to most views, Pelé is the greatest player of all time. Although I never saw him in the flesh, I saw him live on TV, and of course via many of the 1,000s of video clip archives.

However, I believe that Messi may overtake Pelé; many will argue he is a better all round player now. It is certainly a valid argument that Messi displays a greater all-round abundance of skills. But as we cannot see every move or goal that Pelé scored, we cannot make a direct comparison.

However, the main differences I consider most relevant are overall career achievements, so I don't think we can properly judge until Messi's career has ended. In his first eight seasons at Barca, Messi has scored 169 goals in 214 matches. If goals are a valid measure of progress Pelé had scored 295 times in 206 appearances in his first eight seasons.

At club level Pelé helped his team Santos win the Copa Libertadores twice (equivalent of the Champions League) and has 23 various Brazilian domestic league title medals. He also won three Intercontinental cup medals.

Internationally, Pelé made his debut for Brazil at the age of 16, scoring one goal. He immediately became a regular, making 107 appearances, scoring 95 goals. He appeared in four World Cup final tournaments, winning three World Cup winners medals in 1958, 1962 and 1970.

Without doubt Messi will go on to achieve further greatness at both club and international level. However, I don't think that anyone will ever be able to make a direct comparison between what will Messi and Pelé actually achieved.

Firstly, the game has changed so much and it is more difficult to reach the same level of achievement now as it was in the fifties and sixties. Secondly, due to the popularity of Pelé on a global level, Santos travelled the globe to play exhibition matches, so his phenomenal ratio of goals to games cannot ever be directly compared. Incidentally, the records show that Pelé scored 1,246 goals in 1,334 matches for Santos, New York Cosmos and Brazil.

So, having already established that Pelé and Messi are my first two choices, in terms of natural skill, George Best is my third.

This is totally biased as he was British, and I had the privilege of being hypnotised by his mesmerising skills on two occasions.

If George had been able to resist the demon of alcohol, we would have had a prolonged opportunity to witness his sublime skills into the early 80s. It is just such a shame that his exuberant lifestyle affected and subsequently shortened his career, and ultimately his life.

Simply the Best

Just a young lad from Belfast,
To United he was trusted;
A new Busby babe,
Skills jewel encrusted.

With skills we'd never witnessed,
He made defenders look like plums,
Skip past them, spin and dazzle them,
Often left them on their bums.

All football fans adored him,
No matter what they say;
So when he came to town
They packed the ground,
Always keen enough to pay.

The ladies too adored him,
Not quite in the same way;
When he came to town,
They all queued up,
He never had to pay.

George was a footballer
And he liked to tackle hard;
So despite the fancy footwork,
He often saw a card.

George was a playboy
And he liked to party hard;
Despite his magic on the pitch,
Off field an image tarred.

But he still remains a legend,
A true football great;
So cheers Georgie boy,
And thanks for the ride;
And for the millions who saw you play,
Have a drink on us... enjoy!

"*I spent 90% of my money on women, drink and fast cars. The rest I wasted*"

George Best.

Edson Arantes do Nascimento

Just a boy from Brazil
With Portuguese roots,
An infectious smile
And football boots.

In a small south east town
Of three sacred hearts,
Edson was born;
To proud upstanding parents,
Though poverty torn.

They had no idea then
Of their protégée elite,
As Edson would play
With a ball made from socks,
No boots, just bare feet.

His father Dodhino,
A footballer too,
A journeyman type
When they moved to Bauru.

Though Dodhino was good,
It was not much of a living;
It was not a top club
And he was injury struck.

But his coaching paid off
His son soon got the chance,
When at only fifteen,
He was signed up by Santos.

He made his mark for Brazil
At the age of sixteen;
He scored on his debut
A feat rarely since seen.

So naturally gifted,
So naturally blessed,
During this football era
He was surely the best.

He made his mark
With more than 1,200 goals,
As he travelled the world
In a career paved in gold.

An ambassador now
For both football and sport;
A supreme legacy,
An inspiration in boots,
A national treasure
To his country and roots.

Seasonal swings

Perhaps one of the biggest frustrations in supporting a team are the perennial seasonal swings we go through. Even before a new season dawns, we become excited, waiting for the new fixtures in mid to late June, who do we have on the first day, when are the juicy fixtures.

By nature, fans are optimistic types (you have to be on the whole!), but it doesn't take much for early optimism to fade.

Within six weeks of the new season kicking off, our excitement can turn to a resignation that we are probably not going to achieve anything. Some fickle fans even transcend into pessimism before the season starts, for example, if we do not win most of our friendlies or fail to sign a couple of game changing players.

Some fans are lucky. In general, most of the "top six" start well year on year. But for the rest it is always a testing time.

Even if our team are underperforming (in our eyes), we have the minor Cups to make an early mark. For us who support lowly sides, this starts early. A chance to progress on one front at least if the league form isn't all it should be.

Then we go out first or second round. What now? Maybe our league form will pick up (the optimistic trait should instinctively kick in now). If form improves, it keeps us going until Christmas at least. If not, it seems colder and wetter, and the evenings even darker in the late autumn and winter.

A New Season Dawns

It's the eve of the season,
Still warm summer rays,
We return full of hope
In the late evening haze.

The pitch now pristine,
Not a blemish or taint,
And even the barriers
Have a new lick of paint.

The players all tanned,
The manager upbeat,
The chairman waves,
At his team elite.

Can we improve this time round?
Will the new boys fit?
They do look the part
In their new shiny kit.

Everyone's excited,
A friendly with Milan;
But we played like dogs
And lost four nil,
So now what's the plan?

Another Season Over

Another season over,
A time to reflect,
A time to assess;
How we never won more
Is anyone's guess.

Just eight months ago
In the late summer sun,
We set off on our dream
Club united as one.

We started ok,
Two wins and a draw,
But an early cup exit
To a lower league team
Showed a serious flaw.

Then two losses at home,
The confidence just vanished,
Early thoughts of success
Now quickly banished.

By Christmas we knew
Tough times were ahead;
No seasonal presents
From Santa's sled.

The New Year dawned,
When only three wins in nine,
Saw us fall even further
We were becoming supine.

Our strikers goal shy,
The defence looking creaky,
Then in early spring
Something quite freaky;
We won four out of six,
Climbed to tenth just like that;
An air of optimism,
It was no longer flat.

Easter arrived with
Four games in eight days,
But like an egg in the sun,
Optimism soon melted,
A shocking run,
The manager pelted.

With just six games to go
We were close to the drop,
Just two points ahead
Of the teams just below;
Then somehow we rallied,
Beat the team in sixth spot,
Then a fine home draw
To the team at the top.

Just four points now needed
To keep us from trouble.
We won two out of three;
We were safe in the bubble.

Another season over,
Where we didn't achieve;
Where we failed to impress
Nor even get going.

Another season over,
Where early expectations,
Went by the wayside
In a year of frustrations.

And despite all the hype
And the over egged quotes,
It seems nothing has changed,
Where our dreams of promotion
Were simply deranged.

Ups, Cups and Downs

Promotion and relegation, the two ends of the spectrum of our football linked emotions.

Although a win against one of the giants in the cup will incite fervour and even euphoria, it is only second to winning on the last day of the season to secure promotion or a championship. A cup exit to a lowly side, or an abject performance when you are facing relegation, has the opposite effect. I have experienced all of these, but it has probably evened out over my life as a fan, so I can't really complain.

In terms of ups and downs, I have probably experienced more supporting Pompey as the average fan, witnessing four promotions, four relegations, plus off two FA Cup finals, winning in 2008 against Cardiff, and losing in 2010 against Chelsea.

Incidentally, the 2010 FA Cup Final was a bittersweet affair and tested the depth of my emotions. Considering the difference in league position and player personnel, we played defiantly and held them off, despite long periods of Chelsea possession and a barrage of attacks.

In the 54th minute, and still 0-0, we won a penalty. Kevin-Prince Boateng stepped forward to take it. Like many fans around me, it was almost unbearable to watch. If we were to snatch an unlikely victory, this was our chance.

He missed. Four minutes later Drogba scored the winner.

That is football!

What made the occasion even more bittersweet and emotional was that we had already been relegated to the Championship, finishing in bottom place. What's more, the club was yet again in Administration and on the brink of extinction.

As our players came over to applaud the faithful, I welled up. I didn't let out my emotions in a bawling way, but I shed sad tears for the first time ever at a game. I couldn't help it, It just happened. I looked at the players below and the loyal fans around me. I actually thought that this might be the last time I would see my team in the league; I feared liquidation and expulsion from the league.

I remember saying to my friend's son who was next to me, "So what happens now?" He sort of shook his head then looked down, but I could see he had tears in his eyes too.

As previously documented, I started to support Pompey when they were on the verge of relegation. We spent two years in the bottom tier, but that second season was possibly the pinnacle of my fan 'career', certainly in terms of longevity over a whole season.

For a start, the club had turned around somewhat financially. Despite their plight in recent years, they were still a well supported club. At that time our stadium could be considered half decent, certainly as good as any other in that division. We were also (arguably) playing below our level. This meant we could attract decent enough players to help us rise from the basement of the league fairly quickly.

Secondly, I was young and single, earning a reasonable wage. This meant I could afford to watch as many matches as I wanted, home and away. I also worked a shift pattern that allowed me to go to many evening away games without the need to take much time off work.

The first season in Division four was satisfactory. We finished seventh and were unlucky not to finish higher. We only needed two or three more half decent players to seriously challenge next time round.

We signed three players during the close season that would prove pivotal in our 1979/1980 promotion year, in Joe Laidlaw, Terry Brisley and Steve Aizlewood.

In fairness, Aizlewood was brought in to replace Steve Foster, a young and talented centre half who had inevitably departed to a higher standard with Brighton. Steve went on to achieve three full England caps. However, Aizelwood proved a worthy replacement and commanded our defence.

In what was a bit of a roller-coaster ride, we achieved promotion and I went to more matches that season than ever before or since, most with my friend Nick (previously mentioned). There were some great matches and fantastic support to go with it.

We played promotion rivals Bradford City in front of more than 23,800 home fans, winning 4-1. The packed Fratton End sucked in two goals that day. In a period when football attendances were on the decline, that season in Division 4 we achieved twenty three 12,000 plus home crowds including five over 20,000.

When we played Aldershot away towards the end of the season we outnumbered the home fans by three to one. We scored four or more goals nine times at home that season, winning 6-1 on two occasions.

However, the pinnacle of that season was the day we were promoted.

Glory Days

I am sure that all fans experience at least one Glory Day in their life. To some it may not necessarily mean a club history changing event, but it is the day they will never forget, something that conjures up life long memories to relive again and again, especially through long barren spells.

Some fans, specifically those of the "top six", will have more than their fair share of Glory Days. But even then, I would expect that one particular day will stand out more than the others.

For me, it was the third of May, 1980. We were away to Northampton Town and had to win to stand any chance of being promoted. Peterborough also needed to do us a favour by beating Bradford who currently held fourth spot.

It started around 8.30am when I picked up my then girlfriend's brother, Malc, and another mutual friend Terry. As neither of the other two had a car I drove to Northampton. We stopped just north of Newbury for breakfast around 10am. There were four South Coast coaches parked up and we shared breakfast with around two hundred fellow fans. Even then there was a buzz in the air and everyone looked excited, yet I know we all felt apprehensive too.

We arrived at Northampton amongst a convoy of cars and coaches around 12.30. I found a safe place to park just around the corner from a pub we noticed was packed to the brim with Pompey fans. We soon joined them and had a couple of swift pints. Although the pints were swift, we actually spent more time queueing at the bar than it took to drink them. It was fair walk to the County Ground but we arrived there just before two. As expected it was another mammoth away crowd and we queued for nearly forty minutes before finally entering the ground.

It was a very strange venue for football, as it doubled up as the home of Northamptonshire County Cricket Club. The ground only had three sides, the fourth side being completely open due to the size of the cricket field.

The match generally went to plan. We dominated for long spells and scored a goal in each half. With ten minutes to go, things were still comfortable, then news came through that Peterborough were one up. This led to a spell of communal cheering across the terraces.

Waiting for the final whistle was agony. Reports swept around the ground that the match at Peterborough had finished and Bradford had lost. After having it definitely confirmed by multiple radio armed fans, the agony quickly turned to delirium! Within a minute or so the final whistle blew and fans streamed onto the pitch. Malc, Terry and I remained on the terrace and in a group hug we simultaneously jumped up and down, pumping the air with our spare fists.

After a long ovation to our match day heroes, we began to slowly sift out of the ground. On the way back to the car we decided we should head to London to prolong the celebrations, where a lot of other fellow fans would also surely head.

Traffic was kind and the trip back down the M1 and into London was quick. Before we had left Northampton Malc called his best mate from University, Steve, who lived in Hampstead. Although a Middlesborough fan, he was up for joining us in our celebrations. After picking up Steve we headed for the West End and parked near Leicester Square.

Then one of those stupid happenings occurred, just when you don't want it to.

We found an NCP car park and when we reached the car park barrier the attendant informed us it was very busy with only a couple of spaces. He told us we could leave the car with him to park up. I agreed and he gave me a ticket to reclaim it later.

The others got out and pushed down the car lock button on the passenger side. I did the same but just as the door closed, I realised the key was still in the ignition. I announced this to the other three lads and they looked at me in that way, then laughed. When I told the attendant, he was not amused; another car was behind us now waiting to enter.

The attendant said he would have to break the window as the car had to be moved. I suddenly remembered having been in this situation once before. Then in an instant I recalled how I could unlock it. I told the attendant he was not going to break the window and asked if he had a large screwdriver and metal coat hanger. He scurried off to the small office and luckily, returned with both. He asked what I was going to do with them, to which I replied, unlock it!

I squeezed the screwdriver tip between the door and the roof and carefully managed to prise the door open at the top by about half an inch. Good I thought. Then I mangled the metal coat hanger into a long metal strand, with a small cocked loop at the end. I asked Steve to repeat the process of prising open the door while I fed down the reformed coat hanger. After about three attempts and small adjustments to the loop, I managed to hook it over the lock button and pull it up to the unlock position. I opened the door, then smiled at the attendant returning the screwdriver and mangled coat hanger.

We immediately set off in search of a pub!

I suppose it was about 7.30pm by the time we found a suitable, fan friendly establishment near Leicester Square. We had a great couple of hours there, celebrating with fellow fans and a small contingent of Hull Kingston Rovers fans, who had won the Rugby League Challenge Cup Final at Wembley the same day. I couldn't drink much for obvious reasons, and had to make do with a couple of pints and a few cokes. Malc, Terry and Steve probably downed five pints each but it didn't matter that I couldn't celebrate in the same way, I was still on a high!

Around 9.30pm we decided to go to Trafalgar Square. It was awash with our fans, maybe 200 plus. On the far side of the square there was a smaller contingent of blue clad supporters celebrating, but this turned out to be Leicester fans after they had secured the division two title, winning at Orient.

We joined in the ongoing celebrations and after a few minutes, Terry and I jumped into one of the fountains joining a dozen or so others who were chanting the "Pompey Chimes".

Soaking wet to the waist we left Trafalgar Square and headed back to Leicester Square for a final beer and home. The lads had a couple and we left London around 11pm, still very damp. By now I was really tired and once we left the street lights of outer London on the A3 I began to struggle to keep my eyes open. Malc, Terry and Steve (who had just instinctively jumped into the car with us) had all dozed off.

After ten minutes I had to wake them up to help me keep my mind alert. With this they fired football questions at me for the rest of the journey. We eventually arrived back in the Portsmouth area at around 12.30am. What a day, my mind was still racing by the time I slipped into bed, but within minutes I was happily asleep.

There was one other 'away day' where the memories will remain with me forever. Although we lost that day it has become folklore amongst the thousands of fans who made the journey. It happened the following season.

In late August I went with my by then partner, Malc and his partner, for a long weekend in Blackpool, whom we were playing on the Saturday. It's a good place for an away day, we had a great weekend, taking in the lights, the big rides at the fair, messing about on the beach and frequenting some lively pubs.

After lunch on Sunday we set off for home, but decided to venture into Liverpool on the way back, a city we had never visited. Our objective was to have a peek at Goodison Park and Anfield. We stopped outside the impressive Anfield stadium with its Shankly iconic gates.

Malc and I both agreed that it would be something else should we ever have the opportunity to see our team play there one day. Barely two months later, it seemed fate had answered our wishes. In Round 4 of the League Cup, we were drawn with Liverpool, away!

October 28th 1980 was a momentous day. We made up nearly half of the 32,000 attendance when more than 14,000 fans ascending on Anfield for a Tuesday evening fixture. For half an hour before kick-off we sang loud and non-stop. The team received a very loud tickertape welcome and the singing continued through the whole match, apart from a short three minute spell at half time.

We went 1-0 down after 23 minutes, but then our lowly division three side rocked Anfield when we equalised fourteen minutes later. An unbelievable roar of 14,000 fans in unison, followed by the Pompey chimes. We had out-sung the normally vivacious Kop all night, including a loud rendition of "You'll never walk alone" late in the game, thousands of scarves aloft. At this point the Kop applauded; it was for the support and passion we showed on the night.

The 4-1 defeat didn't matter. We played manfully and the final score flattered Liverpool.

After the match we headed into the city. We found the Cavern and then a great friendly pub called the Old Post Office. We started discussing the match with a few Liverpool fans. One guy who had been in the Kop that night told us that during that silent moment at half time a fellow Scouser loudly quipped "Will someone put another shilling in the Juke Box please!"

I have witnessed many other unforgettable matches and impressive fan passion. I consider myself lucky in that I have been there to savour most of my teams great moments over the last thirty five years. I have also savoured some dire moments too, but I think all in all, the good times far outweigh the bad times.

A Different Emotion – United in Grief

Whatever anyone outside of the game thinks, football fans are not mindless simpletons who have nothing better to do. These people annoy me when they make fickle remarks about something they know little about.

It is even more annoying to see the number of what I call "plastic fans" who attend games. The ones hosted on a corporate jolly, who claim to be football fans, but who know very little about the game beyond a goal being scored.

True fans have a united passion for a game we enjoy and love. A bi-product of that passion is a team, whether it's the one you follow week in week out, or your national team. We adapt a deep sense of fierce loyalty to the team we support. It is a similar loyalty that most people have to their family.

We also unite in another way, grief. We have all seen this, commonly to observe a minutes' silence or a slow hand clap for a former player or great of the game who has recently died.

However, the most intense display of fans united in grief follows a football related disaster. The Hillsborough disaster in 1989, when 96 Liverpool fans lost their lives, signifies this more than any other event.

After the disaster I remember it being a sad discussion point with other fans for weeks. No sick jokes were made and every true football fan would have related to the disaster, invoking emotional thoughts for the 96 who died.

Hillsborough, 15th April 1989

So many suffered
At the hands of a few;
It never should have happened,
It could have been prevented;
But it wasn't.

For the ninety six,
Justice was sought;
But they lied and concealed;
The truth never admitted.

Twenty three years on
The truth is still out there;
It will never likely be found,
But memories for those who died
Will always live on.

Fabrice

I was watching the game,
It happened, so quick;
It seemed surreal,
You fell like a brick.

I just couldn't believe
What was actually unfolding,
My heart in my mouth,
As my head I was holding.

Before your fall
You were standing so tall;
How could such a young man
Just hit the wall.

But thankfully Fabrice,
You were strong,
And pulled through,
And I hope it's not long,
'til you pull on your shirt

Is the "bubble" bursting?

Over the past 40 years we have gradually moved from a golden era of football, dictated by events on the field, to one that is now driven by profit, TV schedules, and quite frankly, corporate greed.

Whilst the quality of football today is truly wonderful, I share an opinion that the sheer volume of financial investment required to achieve greatness is unsustainable.

I am not saying that in the past all football clubs were financially fine and dandy; South Shields (1930), Accrington Stanley (1962) went out of business due to financial problems. However, they were rare 'one-offs' caused by extraordinary circumstances. More recently Charlton (1984) and Middlesborough (1986) were liquidated, but were thankfully reformed.

However, by the late eighties a trend of English league clubs entering Administration had set in. This accelerated through the nineties, when sixteen clubs fell into Administration. Then between 2001 and 2009 a further thirty clubs suffered the same fate. All of the English league clubs during this period have survived in one form or another. Since 2010 another six clubs have faced liquidation. At the point of writing this book Portsmouth, Port Vale and Darlington are currently in Administration with no bids to buy the clubs formally accepted as yet.

Scottish clubs have also faced the same problem since 2000, although not on the same scale. However, both Airdrieonians and Gretna became defunct. But it is the plight of Rangers FC that has rocked the foundations of British football.

Rangers Football Club entered into Administration on February 14th 2012 as a result of a tax dispute with HMRC where significant payment irregularities were disclosed. Rangers were forced to liquidate on June 14th after failure to reach a CVA agreement with HMRC.

Although they have re-formed under a new company they face an uncertain future. At this point they are not even sure which division of the Scottish league they will be playing in when the 2012/2013 season kicks off. The impact of Rangers reforming has also had direct implications on a number of other Scottish clubs. It has been reported that several SPL clubs are on financial 'amber alert', due to the loss of gate receipts and TV earnings by not playing Rangers.

The whole issue around Rangers is a mess and clearly outlines the fragile financial state that football has managed to create for itself. As a football fan supporting a club in similar circumstances, I really feel for the 100,000 plus true Rangers fans.

In researching for this book I have spoken to a few true Blues; they feel let down by the SPL, the Scottish FA, but most of all by the shenanigans of the former owner(s).

How can a club with Rangers' pedigree, who were reported to be a 'rich club' some years earlier, fall into such a financial abyss? I suspect gross mismanagement, and like my own club I also suspect there are some who have lined their pockets at the expense of the club's demise.

The case of Rangers and the other clubs in financial difficulties could be the tip of the iceberg. As the richer clubs dominate further, it puts more pressure on the smaller clubs to compete and survive. More clubs than ever are showing signs of financial frailty, and not just small clubs either.

Further recent press rumours speculate that eight current and former English Premier League clubs have significant tax payment issues, i.e. tax bills outstanding. But it isn't just unpaid tax related implications that can put a club in trouble.

Although this thought is a hypothetical scenario, what if an owner of a big six club, like Chelsea, decided to throw their toys out of the pram and just up and go. We know, to sustain the challenge as a top four club a lot of personal investment is thrown into the pot. But if the owner decided he or she had had enough and sold up cheaply, and no one with anywhere near the same level of money to invest came in, how would they fare?

Would they be able to afford the wages, the tax bills and investment needed to remain a top side? Would they just become a mediocre team who couldn't really compete for top honours, facing occasional relegation dog fights? Or would they struggle irrecoverably?

I fear that the Rangers scenario and the predicament that others in Administration are currently facing will become more prevalent in the next three to five years; possibly a domino effect that could affect even the most modest, grass roots supporters.

Is the bubble about to burst for many famous clubs like Rangers? or will sensibility prevail and the football authorities and clubs themselves come up with a sustainable model that prevents any reasonably well run club suffering the possibility of being wound up? I hope so.

Portsmouth Football Club 1898 – 2012 (Pompey forever)

Gentleman Jim must be looking down,
His face in anguish under a worried frown;
Cliff there too now, I hope they can speak
And damn the mess that those did wreak.

They fooled us with Premier League success,
But the spending spree was far in excess
Of a club with no big four aspiration
Debts growing fast, throughout the duration.

A new ground was announced, a digger arrived
With Milan at the wheel, it was cleverly contrived;
But no ground emerged, it was simply a front
It fooled us all; a cheap publicity stunt.

Yes, there were great times and fine players too,
The fans came in droves, an army of blue,
On cloud nine in the cup, two thousand and eight,
Little known then of the club's troubled state.

We were the new Wembley kings, five times in two years;
Then two thousand and ten, our hopes turned to fears.
Stories emerged of our financial plight:
Administration, points deducted, no more top flight.

New owners came in, but it again turned to dust,
Like our decaying stanchions, turning to rust.
Mindless mismanagement to a disturbing degree,
Perpetrators now gone; and what more, scot free.

No legacy was left, just this crippling debt
Relegation yet again, but worse I suspect,
Again on the verge of liquidation,
Again, the laugh of the nation.

But the tradition, the history, will always live on;
Proud Pompey, the fans, will never be gone;
And if we need to reform, well that has to be;
But we will rise again, just wait and see!

PUP

The Money-Go-Round

Our clubs, our league, no longer our own,
So very different to what we had known.

A monopoly of our national sport
Subscription TV in order to fleece.
The Murdoch steamroller started it all;
Then rich foreign investors came in for a piece.

They sold out to the Premier League,
Ruling the schedules and how we watch;
With prices reflecting the owners' needs,
For a millionaire lifestyle and shiny yacht.

Foreign player filled teams
Costing millions in fees;
For a mind boggling wage
They strut out of the tunnel
And onto their stage.

I fear for our game
And I fear for some clubs,
Facing a future so bleak
If they don't find a sheik.

We need to do something
To put out these fires,
Before our national game
Chokes and expires.

Football Talk (rabbit rabbit)

This section looks at the language side of our game, be it the quirkiness of our diverse football dialect, to the often quaint nicknames we use for our clubs.

I do sometimes wonder how the quirky jingoistic phrases we hear came about. What was actually going through the mind of the person who was the first to use a particular phrase? Did they plan it, or did it just spring into their head as they were being interviewed? Personally, I suspect the latter. I also suspect, in some cases, it was contrived as a joke, like "sick as a parrot"; this particular phrase possibly stemmed from the famous Monty Python (Norwegian Blue) parrot sketch of the 70s.

Joking apart, I am sure we have all sporadically spluttered out stupid or funny things, but they are usually the result of genuine mistakes, like a spoonerism or mispronunciation, when our mouth is operating too fast for our brain.

Despite the origins, I have listed many of the commonly used phrases that have been bandied around by various high profile personnel in the football industry. After each one I have tried to convey how they may actually be interpreted and responded to by a non football fan.

Before leading into that, a couple of related poems, the first being a very, very short verse about our esteemed pundits on the TV!

The TV Tarts

On TV and looking cool,
They think they know it all.
End of.

Literally Speaking or Not

It makes me smile and often laugh,
It sometimes makes me wince;
The verbal spew
And ineloquent quotes
Of the post match interview.

The managers, the players,
The commentators too,
Even the pundits possess this spiel
And speak this déjà vu.

So I hope you enjoy this sideways look
At the clichés we often hear.
It's just tongue in cheek,
In salute of that clique
And their language so unique.

It's the way they tell 'em!

"The gaffer set the stall out before the match"
What? You had a jumble sale before the match? And if you did, surely he would delegate that task to one of the junior players or administration staff.

"We have to get a result tomorrow"
Well, for sure you will. A win, a draw and a loss is actually classed as a "result".

"They're too good to go down"
Well they obviously won't then.

"We were shocking, it was men against boys"
You should really sign on men then, otherwise you should expect to lose by 8-0 or more, every week.

"It was a game of two halves"
It always is, one half of 45 minutes, a break, then another of 45 minutes, plus any additional time the referee adds on. Am I missing something here?

"There are no easy games in this league"
I would suggest you play in a lower league then, make it a bit easier on the poor players.

"We weren't hungry enough"
What, you mean for the half time biscuits or post-match sandwiches? If so, you really should have had a smaller pre-match lunch.

"We do our talking on the pitch"
You mean you don't talk off field? No verbal coaching pre-match or half time tactical discussions? You obviously have to shout all the time then as the players can sometimes be 100 yards away, let alone the noise of the crowd.

"It was the worst possible start"
I would have thought that the referee awarding the opposition a ten goal start would be worse.

"We couldn't settle early doors"
Hire a proper tradesman then, you can't expect football players to be able to hang doors, whether delivered early or late.

"We didn't test the keeper"
Well, if not too late, you can always call in a teacher and conduct the test straight after the match.

"They showed real passion out there"
What? Lots of kissing (with tongues?), I bet the opposition were pretty wary of getting too close, good tactics!

"Obviously they're a good side"
Obviously, you just lost 5-0

"We have to take one game at a time"
It's not really practical to play two matches simultaneously, but I suppose if you have a very large squad and mixed and matched the players, it could potentially be achieved.

"He's unplayable at the moment"
Why play him then?

"He holds the ball up well"
I'm not surprised, he has arms the size of prize marrows.

"He runs his socks off"
Surely if he wears football boots, they can't just come off. Alternatively, try those elasticated hold-ups, or even tape to keep them on, which is the norm.

"He's got a great engine"
What? Like a BMW, or other such motor propelled machine? Is that fair?

"He's on fire at the moment"
Well, don't just stand there talking, put a fire blanket over him and call the fire brigade! If it happens often, make sure you always have an extinguisher and fire blanket readily available.

"He has a cultured left foot"
I assume by this you mean his left foot has been artificially nurtured in some way, is that fair?

"He has a good touch for a big lad"
You should appoint him as the club masseur then.

"In the Premier League it's a different proposition when you're up against your Rooneys, your Ronaldos, your Gerrards and your Lampards..."
I honestly don't remember any other players in the Premier League with those names.

What's in a name?

It must seem very odd
To those outside the game;
A British eccentricity
Why we have another name.

But the roots run deep,
There's an underlying reason,
Why these names have stood,
For season after season.

And though it's just a nickname,
Each has historic meaning;
It's inherent to our game,
Not just eccentric leaning.

Be it Rovers or United,
The Tykes or the Toon,
Cheered on by their fans
Each Saturday afternoon.

The Quakers or the Shakers,
The County or the Tayn,
Supported thick and thin
Through snow, wind and rain.

The Peacocks or the Owls,
The Gulls or the Gills,
Followed up and down the land
Through valleys, over hills.

The Tigers or the Lions,
The Stags or the Bulls,
Real people, loyal fans
Through good times and the falls.

The Pilgrims or the Pirates,
The Hornets or the Bees,
Different types of people
Just like chalk and cheese.

The Eagles or the Seagulls,
The Canaries or the Magpies,
True fans through and through,
Where passion never dies.

The Bantams and the Foxes,
They won't mix too well,
And what the hell are Baggies?
Ask me and I'll tell.

The Clarets or the Irons,
The Shots or the Latics,
Collecting every programme,
For storing in their attics.

Third Image "Victor the Magpie" © Copyright Matthew Wilkinson

PASSION UNITED

The Imps, Shrimps or Robins,
And lots of Reds and Blues,
There week in week out,
Win, draw or lose.

The Poppies or the Cherries,
The Daggers or the Blades,
No matter what the league,
The passion never fades.

There are Saddlers, Millers and Minster Men,
Even Posh fans and the Royals,
All walks of life together,
Contrasting, different foils.

Last Word – Modern Day Antics

Diving and other cynical similar forms of antics started to creep into the game in the seventies. It was a style of play 'invented' by our continental counterparts, and while not really evident in Britain back then, it has unfortunately become an inherent part of the professional game globally.

Many modern footballers think nothing of feigning injury to gain advantage, i.e. to win a free kick in a dangerous position or trying to con the referee into sending off an opposing player. As a fan who has also played football at a decent level, I find these antics inexcusable.

I have even seen players in my team take a dive, and when they have it can almost be embarrassing to watch, so you make a joke about it. At the end of the day footballers are actually strong, super fit athletes.

I banter a fair bit with a particular pub mate who is an avid rugby fan. Because of the way the game has changed, it gives rugby fans the chance to ridicule our players (and therefore our game) that they didn't have in the distant past. Bluntly put, they class footballers as overpaid, cheating cissies.

To some extent I have to partially accept this one way banter from real rugby fans, as in general rugby is more honest and played in a 'real man' fashion. Mind you, if I am confronted by a rugby fan that I have not bantered with before, I only have to mention the Harlequins' "bloodgate" scandal to abate their keenness to relentlessly pick on football.

I have watched some rugby at youth level, and it's pretty physical. Even at a young age, when the tackles are hard, they just wince a little then get on with it. If some of today's footballers took a hit like some of these youngsters they would be rolling around in agony. It would give a lot of footballers something to think about if they were made to watch a good hard rugby match.

Although used to varying degrees, diving now seems to be a natural part of a players skill set. I am not sure whether they are coached how and when to dive, but I reckon that someone could make some decent money giving private tuition to the top players on how to make deceptive dives!

In my opinion diving has become prevalent in the game today because of the financial stakes and the huge financial rewards that players receive. Therefore, this 'greed' has overtaken the once sporting and gentlemanly values that the players of yesteryear adhered to.

I do not know what modern players earn in win or performance bonuses, but I bet it is not peanuts. Therefore, in the modern day players' eyes, the team must win at all costs. If feigning injury to eke out time, or diving to gain a goal attempt opportunity from a free kick or penalty can help ensure a victory, and ultimately an extra few thousand in their pay packet, then they will do it.

In my view, there is only one way to stamp out this form of cheating. The players, coaches and football club owners are not going to voluntarily help to eradicate it, even if they do not personally agree with it; the stakes and costs for winning and losing are just too high. Only Footballs' governing bodies and authorities have this power; in the main, this is FIFA.

Referees also have a part to play, but they can only be effective if the laws are changed to allow them to enforce it. Even then, the referees face a difficult task deciding whether cheating has actually occurred, and some referees would not be strong enough to enforce it, giving in to player pressure during the intensity of a match.

I believe the only way to stamp it out once and for all is retrospective punishment, backed up by video evidence. It is so, so simple!

Basically, if video evidence conclusively proves a player has dived or feigned an injury to gain an unfair advantage, the player should be retrospectively banned for three matches and have a fine of one week's salary (or similar) imposed. The club should also be fined an equivalent amount to ensure the coaches stamp it out at the training ground level.

Well, that's just about it, my book on football in my eyes. One last thing though, related to some of the aspects of football that are not quite so good, I decided to write a letter.

It goes something like this...

PASSION UNITED

Dear Santa (Sepp),

It's coming up to Christmas and I have been a good fan all year. I have supported my team through thick and thin again this year, although mostly it has been thin. But above all, I am a fan of football, not just a fan of my team. I have watched other teams on television and the Euros too.

So, in this respect, I hope you can see to it and bring my wishes true as Christmas presents. I only have four and have listed them in order of priority. If I found just a couple of them in my stocking on Christmas morning, I would be very happy.

1) Can you help to introduce a ceiling on transfer fees and players wages, at a global level. I know this may sound a bit of a draconian measure, but quite frankly, paying £50 million in transfer fees and then £150,000 a week in wages is too excessive in anyone's book. It is this reason why so many 'real' fans like me cannot afford to go to matches to support their team.

   Recently, a friend of mine had to pay £53 for his ten year old boy to go and watch 'his team'. He just cannot afford to do this on a regular basis, so the boy will just grow up to be a TV supporter. Instead of him and 1000s of others boys like him, the stadium will be full of rich, corporate types. In years to come, there will be very few children going to watch the big clubs who pay exorbitant transfer fees and wages to players.

2) Please introduce a law or rule to deal with players who 'dive'. I mean fake diving to win a penalty or dangerous free kick, when the player hasn't been touched or only literally brushed, where they end up fooling the ref into giving the free kick or penalty.

3) This is a similar present to above, so it should be easy to sort out. Please introduce a law or rule to deal with players who 'feign' injury to seek advantage. I mean like a player who goes past an opposing

player and hasn't been touched, but ends up rolling around and clutching at their leg or head, or some other part of their anatomy, in order to waste time or even get the other player sent off.

4) Finally, please can you help my national team, England, to win a World Cup? We brought this beautiful game to the world, but we have unfortunately let most of the other nations become too good for us. There are two ways you can help us to restore unity:

   a) Let Britain host a World Cup at the next available opportunity. It needs to 'come home'. By Britain I mean a joint hosted tournament with Scotland, Wales and Northern Ireland. That would be so cool!

   I know you have a strained relationship with our own football association, but let bygones be bygones, and at this seasonal time of goodwill, bury the hatchet once and for all.

   b) If you can sort the hosting of the World Cup to be in Britain, can you outlaw styles of play that our British national teams cannot adapt to?

With home advantage and playing at the same level, we would surely have a chance.

I know I have asked for a lot, but I really think these presents will help the game of football to become a better sport, both on and off the field.

It is so important that the game is made accessible to any fan who wants to go to watch football and support their chosen team.

After all, it's the passion of the fans that makes the game what it is.

Thank you Santa (Sepp),

Love, Philip.

~ THE END ~

Acknowledgements

Many thanks to all of the kind people who have allowed me to use their photo images in this book. Whilst some are public domain or my own photographs, the following people have provided me with permission to reproduce their original images, either directly, or via a Creative Commons free to reproduce or distribute license.

"Page 3 "Match Ready" Copyright Richard Hannam, cameraflair.co.uk (photo by Richard Hannam, kindly reproduced with permission).

Page 7 "Ibrox Flats from train,Glasgow" © Copyright Alex Boyd (photo by Alex Boyd via Flickr, 2007, kindly reproduced with permission).

Page 7 "London Bus" Licensed for use under Creative Commons 2.0, © copyright Adrian Short (Flickr).

Page 15 "Boleyn Ground, West Ham United" Licensed for use under Creative Commons 2.0, © copyright Tom Cuppens (Flickr).

Page 15 "Rangers Fans in the Queue" Licensed for use under Creative Commons 2.0, © copyright Tom Brogan (Flickr).

Page 15 "Crowd" © Copyright Trevor Fletcher (photo by Trevor Fletcher via Flickr, kindly reproduced with permission).

Page 24 "Tottenham warm up" Licensed for use under Creative Commons 2.0, © copyright Sachab (Flickr).

Page 34 "Sunderland Fans 1" Licensed for use under Creative Commons 2.0, © copyright Ronnie MacDonald (Flickr).

Page 37 "The Wheatsheaf, Altrincham" Images © Matthew Wilkinson 2012. All Rights Reserved (photo by Matthew Wilkinson via Flickr, kindly reproduced with permission).

Page 44 "Referees Opinon" © Copyright Richard Burley (photo by Richard Burley kindly reproduced with permission).

Page 46 "Confirmation?" Images © Matthew Wilkinson 2012. All Rights Reserved (photo by Matthew Wilkinson via Flickr, kindly reproduced with permission).

Page 46 "IMG_5568" Licensed for use under Creative Commons 2.0, © copyright Ingy The Wingy (Flickr).

Page 46 "IMG_5552" Licensed for use under Creative Commons 2.0, © copyright Ingy The Wingy (Flickr).

Page 52 "Flag" Licensed for use under Creative Commons 2.0, © copyright Paul Reynolds (Flickr).

Page 52 "Hope" Licensed for use under Creative Commons 2.0, © copyright Ethan Kan (Flickr).

Page 52 "IMG_1663kl" Licensed for use under Creative Commons 2.0, © copyright Agnieszka Lapinska (Flickr).

Page 52 "Remains" Licensed for use under Creative Commons 2.0, © copyright PetrasGagilas (Flickr).

Page 57 "Old Wembley Towers" Licensed for use under Creative Commons 2.0, © copyright Nick (Flickr).

Page 62 "Soccer All Star Lionel Messi" Licensed for use under Creative Commons 2.0, © copyright Rafael Amado Deras (Flickr).

Page 63 George Best photographs kindly reproduced with permission from the owner of a private collection of original George Best photographs.

Page 64 George Best photograph kindly reproduced with permission from the owner of a private collection of original George Best photographs.

Page 65 "Tres Coracoes" Licensed for use under Creative Commons 2.0, © copyright Milton Jung.

Page 66 Pele photograph – public domain.

Page 66 "Pele" Licensed for use under Creative Commons 2.0, © copyright Des Byrne.

Page 79 "030" Licensed for use under Creative Commons 2.0, © copyright Nathan17.

Page 82 Liverpool 96 Licensed for use under Creative Commons 2.0, original © Copyright unspecified.

Page 84 "Gretna" © Copyright Gordon McCreath (photo by Gordon McCreath via Flickr 2012, kindly reproduced with permission).

Page 85 "John Greig Statue" © Copyright Gordon McCreath (photo by Gordon McCreath via Flickr 2012, kindly reproduced with permission).

Page 85 "Ibrox Gates" © Copyright MikeyInMotion (photo by MikeyInMotion via Flickr 2012, kindly reproduced with permission).

Page 89 "Arsenal vs Manchester City" Licensed for use under Creative Commons 2.0, © copyright Wonker.

Page 96 "IMG_7575" Licensed for use under Creative Commons 2.0, © copyright Ingy The Wingy.

Page 96 "Gunnersaurus Rex" Licensed for use under Creative Commons 2.0, © copyright Wonker.

Page 96 "Victor the Magpie" Images © Matthew Wilkinson 2012. All Rights Reserved (photo by Matthew Wilkinson via Flickr, kindly reproduced with permission).

Page 96 "Boomer" Licensed for use under Creative Commons 2.0, © copyright Ingy The Wingy.

Page 98 "In Flight" © Copyright Richard Burley (photo by Richard Burley kindly reproduced with permission).

Page 99 "In Emergencies dial 11-1" Licensed for use under Creative Commons 2.0, © copyright Bill Harrison.

Page 100 Sepp Blatter. Photograph reproduced under Creative Commons License 2.0, World Economic Forum.

The following images are included under a general criteria of "No Copyright or source of original image owner found". If under copyright or license, the copyright holder should contact the author.

Page 5 vintage 1960s football photos.

Page 7 Stamford Bridge, 1960s.

Page 10 Shoot Magazine.

Page 18 FA Cup Final Ticket.

Page 32, Football hooligans.

Page 39 Rose Tinted Glasses.

Lightning Source UK Ltd.
Milton Keynes UK
UKOW032309070912

198665UK00001B/7/P